MW00958662

All About Leo Messi

Inspiring stories, facts and trivia about

a soccer superstar

All the history, details and incredible feats you

need to know as a superfan of Leo Messi

ColorCraftBooks.com

Table Of Contents

Claim Your Free Bonus Coloring Book

A free bonus coloring book download is waiting for you as a thank you for picking up this book. We think you'll like it.

Just scan the QR code below or visit
ColorCraftBooks.com/colorcraft-bonus.

Kids: Make sure to ask a parent first! ●

Scan to get your free coloring book download:

Introduction: A Magical Night in Barcelona

Imagine a stadium filled with nearly 100,000 fans eagerly waiting for the biggest match of the year: El Clásico, the epic battle between FC Barcelona and Real Madrid.

The atmosphere is electric, with fans chanting, waving flags, and proudly wearing their team's colors. On this special night, the world would witness something extraordinary.

It was a night that would be remembered forever, thanks to one player: Leo Messi.

In the heart of Barcelona, excitement was building at the famous Camp Nou stadium. Fans knew they were in for a treat whenever Barcelona and Real Madrid faced off, but no one could predict the incredible show that was about to unfold.

As the players warmed up on the field, all eyes were on the little magician, Leo Messi. Even the opposing team knew they had to watch out for him.

The whistle blew, and the game began. From the start, it was clear that this match was going to be intense. Both teams fought hard, displaying amazing skills and determination. The first half was filled with close calls and brilliant plays, but the score remained tied.

As the second half started, the tension in the stadium was palpable. Fans were on the edge of their seats, hoping for a moment of brilliance to break the deadlock. **And then, it happened.**

Leo Messi received the ball near the halfway line with just a few minutes left on the clock. The crowd roared as he took off, weaving through defenders with his trademark speed and agility.

It was as if he had the ball glued to his feet. One by one, he left the Real Madrid players behind, making his way toward the goal. The fans could hardly believe their eyes. Was he going to do it again?

As Messi approached the penalty area, the last defender lunged at him, desperate to stop him.

But Leo was too quick. He dodged the tackle with a swift move, leaving the defender sprawling on the ground.

Now, it was just him and the goalkeeper. The stadium fell silent, everyone holding their breath. Time seemed to slow down as Messi lined up his shot.

Leo Messi struck the ball with a calmness that only the greatest players possess. It flew past the goalkeeper, who could only watch as it sailed into the top corner of the net. An explosion of cheers shattered the silence.

Fans jumped up and down, hugging each other and celebrating wildly. Leo had done it again. He had scored a hat-trick, three incredible goals, in one of the most important matches of the season.

But it wasn't just the goals that made this night so special. It was the way Leo played, with passion, creativity, and joy. He made the impossible look easy, and he did it all with a humble smile on his face.

For Leo, it wasn't just about winning; it was about bringing joy to the fans and sharing his love for the game.

As the final whistle blew, the crowd erupted in applause. Leo Messi was hoisted onto the shoulders of his teammates, the hero of the night.

Fans chanted his name, celebrating the victory and the player who had given them so many unforgettable moments. That night, under the lights of Camp Nou, Leo Messi reminded everyone why he was considered one of the greatest soccer players of all time.

For young fans watching the game, it was a moment of pure inspiration. Seeing Leo Messi perform at such a high level against one of the toughest teams in the world showed them that anything is possible with hard work and dedication.

It didn't matter where you came from or how small you were. What mattered was the size of your heart and your love for the game.

Leo Messi's journey to this magical night wasn't easy. He faced many challenges along the way, from growing up in a small town in Argentina to overcoming a serious medical condition.

But through it all, he never gave up on his dream. He worked tirelessly, honing his skills and pushing himself to be the best he could be. And on nights like this, all that hard work paid off in the most spectacular way.

This book is about the incredible journey of Leo Messi, from his early days in Rosario to his rise as a global soccer icon. It's a story of determination, passion, and the unbreakable spirit of a true champion.

As you read about Leo's life, you'll learn about his challenges, the victories he achieved, and the moments that defined his career.

Get ready to be inspired by the story of a boy who loved soccer and grew up to become one of the greatest players the world has ever seen.

Leo Messi's story is a reminder that with hard work, perseverance, and a little bit of magic, you can achieve your dreams, no matter how big they are.

So, buckle up and get ready to dive into the amazing world of Leo Messi. The journey is about to begin, and it will be unforgettable!

Did you know:

EL CLASICO

El Clásico between FC Barcelona and Real Madrid is one of the most-watched soccer matches, with up to 650 million viewers worldwide.

Chapter 1: Meet Leo: The Soccer Superstar

"You have to fight to reach your dream. You have to sacrifice and work hard for it." – Leo Messi.

When you think about the greatest soccer players in the world, one name always comes to mind: Leo Messi (full name: Lionel Andrés Messi, often known as "Leo").

He's not just a player; he's a superstar, a magician with the ball, and a hero to millions of fans around the globe. But what makes Leo Messi so special? Why has he become such a star? Let's take a closer look at the amazing qualities that have made him a legend in the world of soccer.

First of all, Leo Messi's skills with the ball are out of this world! From a young age, it was clear that he had a natural talent for soccer. He could dribble past defenders like they weren't even there, make perfect passes, and score jaw-dropping goals.

Watching Messi play is like watching a magician perform tricks. He makes the game look effortless, as if he's dancing with the ball. His ability to control and move the ball exactly where he wants it to go is truly amazing.

But it's not just talent that makes Messi a star. What really sets him apart is his hard work and dedication. Even though he was born with incredible talent, he never took it for granted.

He spent countless hours practicing, honing his skills, and pushing himself to be the best. He trained hard every day, always looking for ways to improve.

This dedication to his craft is one of the reasons why he has stayed at the top of his game for so many years.

Leo Messi is also known for being incredibly humble. Despite all his success, he remains down-to-earth and kind. He never boasts about his achievements or acts like he's better than anyone else. Instead, he lets his actions on the field do the talking.

This humility has earned him the respect and admiration of fans, teammates, and even opponents. It's a reminder that true greatness isn't just about talent; it's also about character.

Another reason why Leo Messi is such a star is his sportsmanship. He always plays fair and treats his opponents with respect. Even in the heat of competition, he never loses his cool or resorts to dirty tactics.

He believes in playing the game the right way and setting a great example for young players. His sportsmanship has made him a role model for aspiring soccer players all over the world.

Leo Messi's journey to stardom wasn't easy. He faced many challenges along the way, but he never gave up. One of the biggest obstacles he faced was his growth hormone deficiency.

This medical condition made it difficult for him to grow like other kids his age. But Messi didn't let this stop him.

With the support of his family and his determination to succeed, he overcame this challenge and continued to pursue his dream of becoming a professional soccer player.

Messi's move to Barcelona was a turning point in his career. At just 13 years old, he left his home in Argentina to join FC Barcelona's youth academy, La Masia.

It was a big change, moving to a new country and adapting to a new culture. But Messi embraced the challenge and quickly made a name for himself. His talent and hard work paid off, and he soon began playing for Barcelona's senior team.

Did you know:

UNIQUE WARMUP ROUTINE
Leo Messi has a specific warmup routine that he follows every game. He starts with light jogging, followed by stretching exercises. Then, he practices his dribbling and shooting. This routine helps him get into the right mindset and perform at his best during matches.

Once Messi started playing for Barcelona, he quickly became a superstar! He scored amazing goals, led his team to victory, and helped them win tons of titles. Every time he stepped on the field, it was like watching magic.

He shattered records, collected awards, and became one of the most celebrated players in soccer history.

His success with Barcelona turned him into a household name and a true soccer legend.

But Leo Messi's awesomeness isn't just about soccer. Off the field, he's a superhero too!

Through his foundation, he helps kids in need by providing them with education and healthcare.

He supports many charitable causes, showing generosity and kindness everywhere he goes.

Messi's big heart has made him a hero not just to soccer fans, but to people all around the world.

Did you know:

LANGUAGE SKILLS
In addition to his native Spanish, Leo Messi also speaks Catalan, the regional language of Catalonia, where Barcelona is located. He learned Catalan during his time at La Masia, showing his dedication to embracing the culture of his adopted home.

One of the coolest things about Leo Messi is his pure love for soccer.

Even with all his amazing achievements, he still plays with the same joy and passion he had as a kid. Whether it's a big championship match or just a friendly match, you can see the happiness in his eyes.

This love for the game keeps him motivated and makes him a joy to watch for fans everywhere. Leo Messi is a soccer superstar for so many reasons. His incredible skills, hard work, humility, sportsmanship, and love for the game have all played a part in his success.

He's faced tough challenges and overcome them, setting a great example for young athletes everywhere. His story shows what you can achieve with talent, dedication, and a big heart.

As you dive into Leo Messi's life and career, you'll discover what makes him such a special player. His journey is packed with amazing moments, unforgettable matches, and inspiring achievements. So get ready to be inspired by the story of Leo Messi, the little boy from Rosario who grew up to become a global soccer icon.

Chapter 2: Humble Beginnings in Rosario

"The best decisions aren't made with your mind, but with your instinct." – Leo Messi.

Leo Messi's journey to becoming a soccer superstar began in the small city of Rosario, Argentina. Born June 24, 1987, Leo was the third of four children in the Messi family. His parents, Jorge and Celia, were hardworking and loving, always making sure their children were happy and well-cared for.

Jorge worked in a steel factory, and Celia was a part-time cleaner, but despite their busy schedules, they always found time for family.

Growing up, Leo was a quiet and shy boy, but he had one great passion: soccer. From the moment he could walk, he had a ball at his feet. His older brothers, Rodrigo and Matias, were also soccer fans, and they often played together in the streets and parks of Rosario.

Leo's grandmother, Celia, was one of his biggest supporters. She believed in his talent and would often take him to his early soccer practices. She knew Leo had a special gift and encouraged him to pursue his dreams.

Did you know:

A SWEET TOOTH

Leo Messi has a well-known love for sweets. One of his favorite treats is alfajores, a traditional Argentine cookie filled with dulce de leche. Despite his rigorous training and healthy diet, Messi allows himself these indulgences, especially during holidays and celebrations.

Leo's first soccer club was Grandoli, a local team where his father was a coach. Even at a young age, Leo's talent was undeniable. He was smaller than the other kids, but what he lacked in size, he made up for in skill and determination.

He could easily dribble past defenders and had an uncanny ability to score goals.

His teammates and coaches were amazed by his natural ability, and it was clear that Leo had a bright future ahead of him.

However, Leo's journey wasn't without challenges. When he was just ten years old, he was diagnosed with a growth hormone deficiency.

This medical condition meant that his body didn't produce enough growth hormone, making it difficult for him to grow like other kids his age.

It was a tough time for Leo and his family. The treatment for this condition was expensive, and the Messi family couldn't afford it on their own.

But Leo's parents were determined to help their son. They explored every option, looking for ways to get Leo the treatment he needed. Despite the financial strain, they never gave up hope.

They believed in Leo's talent and knew that with the right support, he could achieve his dreams. Their love and dedication were a constant source of strength for Leo, helping him stay positive and focused on his goals.

Leo's talent soon caught the attention of larger soccer clubs. At the age of eight, he joined Newell's Old Boys, one of the most prestigious clubs in Rosario. It was a big step for young Leo, but he rose to the challenge.

Playing for Newell's, he continued to shine, scoring countless goals and leading his team to victory in numerous matches. His incredible performances earned him the nickname "La Pulga," which means "The Flea" in Spanish, because of his small size and quick movements.

Did you know:

LOVE FOR MILANESA

One of Messi's favorite dishes is milanesa, an Argentine
comfort food similar to a breaded meat cutlet. Despite his
international fame and access to gourmet cuisine, Messi loves
this simple dish that reminds him of home.

Despite his success on the field, Leo never forgot his
roots. He remained close to his family and friends and
never let his early fame go to his head. His grandmother,
Celia, continued to be one of his biggest supporters,
always cheering him on from the sidelines.

Tragically, she passed away when Leo was just ten years old. This was a heartbreaking moment for Leo, but he found strength in her memory. He often dedicated his goals to her, pointing to the sky in her honor after scoring.

The support and love from his family, combined with his natural talent and hard work, helped Leo overcome the difficulties he faced in his early life.

He continued to grow as a player, and his dream of becoming a professional soccer player seemed closer than ever. But Leo's journey was just beginning.

He would soon face one of the biggest challenges of his life: moving to a new country and adapting to a new culture.

Did you know:

TRAVEL ENTHUSIAST

Messi loves to travel, especially to relaxing beach destinations. Some of his favorite spots include Ibiza and the Caribbean, where he can unwind with his family away from the public eye. These vacations are essential for recharging his energy.

When Leo was 13 years old, he was offered a chance to join FC Barcelona's youth academy, La Masia. It was a life-changing opportunity, but it also meant leaving behind everything he knew.

Leo's family bravely decided to move to Spain so he could pursue his dream. It was a difficult transition, but Leo embraced the challenge with the same determination and resilience that had defined his early years.

Leo Messi's early life in Rosario shaped him into the person and player he is today. The love and support of his family, the encouragement from his grandmother, and the challenges he faced and overcame all played a crucial role in his journey.

His story is a testament to the power of hard work, perseverance, and believing in your dreams, no matter how big they are.

As you read more about Leo's incredible journey, you'll see how his early experiences helped him become one of the greatest soccer players in the world. His story is a source of inspiration for young athletes everywhere, showing that with passion and dedication, anything is possible.

Chapter 3: A Budding Star in Newell's Old Boys

"I start early, and I stay late, day after day, year after year. It took me 17 years and 114 days to become an overnight success." – Leo Messi.

Leo Messi's journey from a young soccer enthusiast in Rosario to a budding star in the world of soccer truly began during his years at Newell's Old Boys. Between the ages of 10 and 16, Leo faced numerous challenges that tested his determination and resilience.

These formative years were crucial in shaping him into the exceptional player he would become.

When Leo joined Newell's Old Boys at the age of eight, his talent was already evident.

His incredible dribbling skills, speed, and goal-scoring ability dazzled his coaches and teammates.

Despite his small stature, he played with a heart full of passion and a mind full of soccer intelligence. However, Leo's path to stardom was not without obstacles.

Did you know:

UNIQUE SUPERSTITIONS

Messi follows a few superstitions before games. For example, he always steps onto the field with his right foot first and often kisses a small pendant given to him by his mother. These rituals help him feel prepared and focused for the game ahead.

One of Leo's biggest challenges was his growth hormone deficiency, which hindered his growth and made competing tough.

The costly treatment was a financial strain, but his parents, Jorge and Celia, worked tirelessly to fund it, believing in his potential. Leo found inspiration and support from his father, Jorge, and his coach, Ernesto Vecchio.

Jorge Messi: A Father's Unwavering Support

Jorge Messi played a pivotal role in Leo's development as a soccer player. Not only was he Leo's father, but he was also his first coach and mentor. Jorge worked long hours at the steel factory to provide for his family, but he always made time to support Leo's soccer ambitions. He would take Leo to practices and matches, offering guidance and encouragement along the way.

Jorge's belief in Leo's talent was unwavering, and his dedication to helping his son succeed was a source of immense strength for Leo.

Jorge taught Leo the importance of hard work, discipline, and perseverance. He encouraged Leo to stay focused on his goals, even when faced with adversity. Jorge's support and belief in his son's abilities were instrumental in helping Leo overcome the challenges he faced due to his growth hormone deficiency.

With his father's guidance, Leo learned to never give up, no matter how difficult the journey seemed.

Did you know:

BIGTIME SCORER
Messi scored over 230 goals for Newell's youth teams between ages six and 13, as a star of the "Machine of '87," a dominant academy team named after the players' birth year.

Ernesto Vecchio: The Coach Who Saw Potential

Ernesto Vecchio, one of Leo's youth coaches at Newell's Old Boys, also played a significant role in his development.

Vecchio recognized Leo's exceptional talent from a young age and believed that he had the potential to become one of the greatest players in the world. He provided Leo with the technical training and tactical knowledge he needed to excel in the field.

Under Vecchio's guidance, Leo's skills flourished. He learned to read the game, anticipate his opponents' moves, and make split-second decisions. Vecchio's coaching style emphasized creativity and freedom on the field, allowing Leo to express himself through his play.

This approach helped Leo develop his unique playing style, characterized by his quick dribbling, precise passing, and incredible vision.

Vecchio's belief in Leo's potential was a tremendous source of motivation for the young player. He encouraged Leo to push his limits and strive for greatness.

Vecchio's mentorship was instrumental in helping Leo build the confidence he needed to overcome his physical challenges and excel on the field.

As Leo continued to develop as a player, he began to attract attention from larger clubs. His performances at Newell's Old Boys were nothing short of spectacular. He scored countless goals, led his team to victories, and became known for his extraordinary talent.

His nickname, "La Pulga," (the flea) became widely recognized as he dazzled fans and opponents alike with his skillful play.

At 13, Leo faced one of the biggest decisions of his young life. FC Barcelona, one of the most prestigious soccer clubs in the world, offered him a chance to join their youth academy, La Masia.

It was an opportunity that could change his life forever, but it also meant leaving behind his home, family, and friends in Rosario.

The decision to move to Barcelona was not an easy one. It required immense courage and determination. Leo's family decided to make the move with him, uprooting their lives to support his dream.

The transition was challenging, as Leo had to adapt to a new country, language, and culture. But his passion for soccer and his unwavering belief in his abilities kept him focused.

Did you know:

COLLECTING JERSEYS
Messi has a vast collection of soccer jerseys from players he has faced throughout his career. His collection includes jerseys from famous players like Ronaldinho, Francesco Totti, and Zinedine Zidane. This collection reflects his respect and admiration for his peers.

At La Masia, Leo's talent continued to shine. He quickly rose through the ranks, impressing coaches and teammates with his skill and dedication.

Leo's determination and love for the game drove him to succeed despite being far from home. He faced tough competition and rigorous training, but he never gave up.

Leo Messi's journey from a young boy in Rosario to a rising star in Barcelona was marked by hard work, resilience, and the support of his loved ones. His challenges during his formative years helped him develop the strength and determination that would define his career.

With the guidance of his father, Jorge, and the mentorship of his coach, Ernesto Vecchio, Leo overcame obstacles and blossomed into the extraordinary player the world knows today.

As you continue to read about Leo's incredible journey, you'll see how these early experiences laid the foundation for his success. His story is a testament to the power of perseverance, the importance of believing in oneself, and the impact that supportive role models can have on a young athlete's life.

Chapter 4: Rising to Stardom: The Young Prodigy

"I try to use pressure to help me in every game. Pressure helps me do things to the best of my ability." – Leo Messi.

By the time Leo Messi turned 16, he was already making waves in the soccer world. His journey from Rosario to Barcelona was full of challenges, but his talent, determination, and family support helped him overcome every obstacle. Now, it was time for Leo to step into the professional arena.

At 16, Leo made his debut for FC Barcelona's senior team in a friendly match against Porto. This young boy, barely old enough to drive, stepped onto the field with some of the best players and shone brightly.

His quick feet, incredible ball control, and sharp instincts left everyone in awe. It was clear that Leo was a special talent.

PET LOVER

Leo Messi has a special place in his heart for animals, especially dogs. He has a massive Dogue de Bordeaux named Hulk, who is often seen in family photos. Messi enjoys spending his downtime playing and relaxing with Hulk, showing that even superstars love their pets.

In October 2004, at just 17 years old, Leo made his official debut in La Liga, Spain's top professional league. He came on as a substitute against Espanyol, becoming the youngest player to play for Barcelona in a league match.

The soccer world quickly took notice of this young prodigy from Argentina with a magical touch.

The next year, in May 2005, Leo scored his first goal for Barcelona in a match against Albacete. At just 17, he became the youngest player ever to score for the club.

The crowd erupted in cheers, and this was just the beginning of his amazing career filled with record-breaking achievements.

Leo's incredible performances caught the media's attention, making him a household name.

He appeared on magazine covers, sports shows, and news articles. Despite all the fame, Leo stayed humble and focused on his game, always working hard to improve.

Did you know:

VIDEO GAME FAN

Messi enjoys playing video games in his free time. He particularly loves playing FIFA, the popular soccer video game. It's a fun way for him to relax and connect with friends and family, even playing as himself in the game!

One of the biggest milestones in Leo's early career came in 2005 when he played in the FIFA U-20 World Cup. Representing Argentina, Leo dazzled everyone with his dribbling, vision, and goal-scoring skills.

He led Argentina to victory, winning the Golden Boot as the top scorer and the Golden Ball as the best player.

This incredible achievement cemented his status as a rising star in world soccer.

As Leo moved from the youth ranks to the senior team, his impact on the field grew. In the 2005-2006 season, he became a regular starter for Barcelona. Whether dribbling past defenders, making precise passes, or scoring stunning goals, Leo was a joy to watch and quickly became a fan favorite.

The media couldn't get enough of Leo Messi. His story of triumph over adversity and mesmerizing play on the field made headlines. He was featured in countless interviews, sharing his journey, dreams, and love for soccer. Despite his growing fame, Leo stayed grounded, always crediting his family, coaches, and teammates for their support.

One of the most iconic moments of Leo's early career came in a 2006 Champions League match against Chelsea. The game was intense, and Leo was at his best, showcasing his dribbling skills and creating numerous scoring opportunities.

Although Barcelona didn't win, Leo's performance earned him widespread acclaim, proving he could compete with the best players on the biggest stage.

As Leo's career progressed, so did his achievements. In 2006, he helped Barcelona win both the La Liga title and the UEFA Champions League. At just 19 years old, he had already accomplished what many players could only dream of, contributing immensely to his team's success and being celebrated as one of soccer's brightest talents.

Off the field, Leo's popularity soared. He appeared in advertisements, became the face of various brands, and inspired young athletes worldwide. His humility, hard work, and dedication made him a role model for aspiring soccer players, showing that with talent, perseverance, and the right attitude, anything is possible.

Did you know:

PASSION FOR CHARITY

Leo Messi is deeply committed to charitable work. Through the Leo Messi Foundation, he supports various projects worldwide, focusing on education and healthcare for children. One notable project is funding medical treatment for children with growth hormone deficiencies, something he personally experienced.

Leo Messi's early career was a time of amazing growth, big achievements, and lots of recognition. From his debut at 16 to winning prestigious titles with Barcelona, Leo's journey was packed with unforgettable moments.

His talent, hard work, and humility set him apart and built the foundation for his future success.

As you keep reading about Leo's incredible journey, you'll see how these early years shaped him into the legendary player we know today.

Chapter 5: Taking Over the Game: Leo's Prime Years

"You can overcome anything, if and only if you love something enough." – Leo Messi.

As Leo Messi entered his twenties, he was poised to become one of the greatest soccer players the world had ever seen. He had already shown flashes of brilliance, but the next phase of his career would be truly extraordinary. Leo's prime years were filled with record-breaking achievements, unforgettable moments, and an incredible rise to prominence that left an indelible mark on soccer.

By age 20, Leo was a regular starter for FC Barcelona and was already being compared to some of the greatest players in history. His skill, vision, and ability to score goals from almost any position on the field set him apart. One of his early defining moments came in the 2008-2009 season when he helped lead Barcelona to a historic treble, winning La Liga, the Copa del Rey, and the UEFA Champions League. This incredible achievement solidified his reputation as a world-class player.

During this time, Leo formed an unstoppable partnership with teammates like Xavi Hernandez and Andres Iniesta. Together, they created a style of play known as "tiki-taka," characterized by quick, precise passing and maintaining possession of the ball. This style allowed Barcelona to dominate matches and break down even the toughest defenses. Leo's ability to weave through defenders and create scoring opportunities was a perfect fit for this system, and his chemistry with Xavi and Iniesta was magical to watch.

In the 2009-2010 season, Leo won his first Ballon d'Or, an award given to the best player in the world. It was the first of many, as he would go on to win this prestigious award seven more times throughout his career.

Each Ballon d'Or win was a testament to his incredible consistency and ability to perform at the highest level year after year. These awards not only celebrated his individual brilliance but also his contribution to his team's success.

Leo's prime years were filled with numerous records and milestones. He became Barcelona's all-time top scorer, surpassing legends like Cesar Rodriguez and Laszlo Kubala. In the 2011-2012 season, he set a world record by scoring 91 goals in a calendar year, a feat that seemed almost impossible.

His ability to score goals in various ways – with his left foot, right foot, head, and even free kicks – made him a constant threat to any defense.

But Leo's journey wasn't without challenges. He faced several injuries that could have derailed his career, but his determination and resilience saw him through. In the 2013-2014 season, he suffered a hamstring injury that kept him out for several weeks.

Many wondered if he would be able to return to his best form, but Leo worked tirelessly on his recovery.

His dedication to getting back to full fitness was inspiring, and he returned stronger than ever, leading Barcelona to more victories and titles.

Did you know:

BIG FAMILY MAN

Family is extremely important to Messi. He often spends his free time with his wife, Antonela, and their three sons, Thiago, Mateo, and Ciro. Messi enjoys playing soccer with his kids, creating a joyful and loving environment at home.

One of the most memorable moments of Leo's prime years came in the 2014-2015 season when Barcelona achieved another treble, winning La Liga, the Copa del Rey, and the UEFA Champions League. This time, Leo was part of a legendary attacking trio alongside Neymar and Luis Suarez.

The trio, known as "MSN," was one of the most feared in soccer history. Their combined skill, speed, and understanding on the field made them nearly unstoppable. Together, they scored over 120 goals that season alone, a record for any attacking trio.

Leo faced many rivalries throughout his career, but none were as famous as his rivalry with Cristiano Ronaldo. The two players pushed each other to new heights, with each trying to outdo the other. Their battles in El Clásico, the matches between Barcelona and Real Madrid, were legendary.

Fans around the world tuned in to watch these titanic clashes, where Leo and Ronaldo showcased their incredible talents. While the rivalry was intense, it was also marked by mutual respect. Both players acknowledged that competing against each other made them better.

Leo's dominance on the field also translated into significant sponsorship deals. He became the face of Adidas, one of the biggest sports brands in the world.

His sponsorship deal was one of the largest in history, earning him millions of dollars each year. He also had endorsements with other major brands like Pepsi, Gatorade, and Huawei. These deals not only recognized his greatness as a player but also his global appeal and influence.

Did you know:

ROLE MODEL TO MANY
Leo Messi's impact goes beyond soccer. He is a role model for millions of young fans worldwide. His story of overcoming adversity, his dedication to his craft, and his humility inspire countless people to pursue their dreams and never give up.

Leo Messi's prime years were filled with unmatched success and dominance in soccer. His incredible skill, determination, and humility led to record-breaking achievements, numerous titles, and the admiration of fans worldwide.

Leo's journey shows what hard work, resilience, and love for the game can achieve. His dedication and passion have made him one of the greatest players in soccer history.

Chapter 6: Beyond the Pitch: Family, Philanthropy, and Personality

"I always had a dream to become a professional soccer player, and I always believed in myself." – Leo Messi.

Leo Messi's brilliance on the soccer field is legendary, but there's so much more to him than just his amazing skills. Off the pitch, Leo is a loving family man, a generous helper, and a person with a joyful heart. His life away from soccer is full of love, kindness, and a big desire to make the world better.

Family is super important to Leo. He married his childhood sweetheart, Antonela Roccuzzo, in 2017. Their love story is like a fairy tale—they met as kids in Rosario, and their bond grew stronger over the years.

Antonela has always been there for Leo, supporting him through all the highs and lows of his career. Together, they have three sons: Thiago, Mateo, and Ciro.

Despite his busy schedule, Leo always makes time for his family. He loves playing soccer in the backyard with his kids and taking them to school.

Leo's personality shines through in everything he does. On the field, he plays with joy and passion. His love for the game is clear in every move he makes, whether he's scoring a goal, celebrating with teammates, or dribbling past defenders.

Fans love to see him smile and laugh during matches, and his playful nature makes the game even more fun to watch. He often dances with delight after scoring, showing just how much happiness soccer brings him.

Did you know:

ARTIST AT HEART

Messi has a hidden talent for drawing. During his childhood, he often sketched soccer players and memorable moments from games. While he pursued soccer professionally, his love for art remains a cherished hobby.

Off the field, Leo Messi is as awesome as he is on it! Even with all his fame and success, he stays humble and kind. He treats everyone with respect, from his teammates to his fans. People all around the world admire Leo for his sportsmanship and generosity.

One of the coolest things about Leo is his big heart. In 2007, he started the Leo Messi Foundation, a charity that helps kids get education and healthcare. Thanks to Leo, many schools, hospitals, and sports facilities have been built, giving kids opportunities they wouldn't have had otherwise.

Leo also loves visiting hospitals and spending time with sick children. He brings joy and hope to them with his smiles, autographs, and fun conversations. Meeting their hero is a dream come true for these kids, and Leo's kindness leaves a lasting impression on their hearts.

Did you know:

FRIENDSHIP WITH AGÜERO
Messi shares a close friendship with fellow Argentine soccer star Sergio Agüero. They roomed together during international tournaments and have supported each other both on and off the field. Their friendship is well-known and cherished by fans.

Leo's achievements have also been recognized with numerous honors and awards. In addition to his Ballon d'Or wins, he's won loads of awards and honors, not just for his amazing soccer skills, but also for his big heart and generosity.

You've probably seen him on magazine covers, in commercials, and even in documentaries about his life. Leo's story inspires people everywhere, showing that with talent, hard work, and kindness, anything is possible.

One of the coolest moments in Leo's career was meeting Pope Francis in 2013. Both are from Argentina and share a love for soccer. They talked about using their fame to make a positive impact on the world. This meeting showed Leo's humility and his desire to do good.

Leo's influence goes beyond soccer. He has his own clothing line and works with major brands to raise awareness for important causes. You might have seen him in movies and TV shows where he shares his journey and the lessons he's learned.

Despite his busy life, Leo always stays true to himself. He loves spending time with his family, playing soccer, and helping others. His dedication to his family, his generosity, and his joyful personality make him a beloved figure both on and off the field.

Leo Messi's life off the pitch is as amazing as his achievements on it. His love, kindness, and hard work make him not just a soccer legend but a true hero. As you read more about Leo's incredible journey, you'll see how his character and values have shaped him into the inspiring figure he is today.

Chapter 7: Record Breaker: Trophies and Triumphs

"It took me 17 years and 114 days to become an overnight success." – Leo Messi.

Leo Messi's career is filled with incredible achievements and record-breaking moments that have solidified his status as one of the greatest soccer players ever. From winning prestigious trophies to setting astonishing records, Leo's journey has been nothing short of spectacular. Let's dive into some of the most memorable and impressive milestones of his career.

Major Achievements

1. La Liga Titles Leo Messi has won the La Liga title with FC Barcelona an astonishing 10 times. His contributions to these victories have been immense, with countless goals and assists that have led Barcelona to the top of Spanish soccer.

2. UEFA Champions League Titles Leo has lifted the UEFA Champions League trophy four times. These victories came in 2006, 2009, 2011, and 2015. Each of these triumphs was marked by Messi's incredible performances, including unforgettable goals and assists that helped Barcelona dominate Europe.

3. Copa del Rey Wins Messi has also won the Copa del Rey seven times. This domestic cup competition showcases the best teams in Spain, and Leo's consistent brilliance in these matches has been crucial to Barcelona's success.

Record-Breaking Moments

1. All-Time Top Scorer for FC Barcelona Leo Messi is FC Barcelona's all-time top scorer, with over 670 goals for the club. This incredible record highlights his consistent excellence and his ability to perform at the highest level season after season.

2. Most Goals in a Calendar Year In 2012, Leo set a world record by scoring 91 goals in a single calendar year. This feat is a testament to his extraordinary talent and relentless determination.

3. Most Hat-Tricks in La Liga Messi holds the record for the most hat-tricks in La Liga history, with over 36 hat-tricks. A hat-trick, which is scoring three goals in a single match, showcases his ability to dominate games and change the course of a match single-handedly.

4. Most Ballon d'Or Wins Leo Messi has won the Ballon d'Or eight times. This prestigious award is given to the best player in the world each year, and Leo's multiple wins highlight his sustained excellence and impact on the sport.

Special Games and International Achievements

1. FIFA World Cup Leo Messi has represented Argentina in multiple FIFA World Cups, always putting on a spectacular show. In 2014, he led Argentina to the final, narrowly losing to Germany, but still earning the Golden Ball as the tournament's best player.

The most thrilling moment came in 2022, when Argentina won the World Cup for the second time in history. Messi was the heart and soul of the team, inspiring his teammates with his incredible skills, leadership, and determination.

His unforgettable performances and crucial goals helped secure Argentina's victory, cementing his legacy as one of the greatest players of all time.

2. Copa America In 2021, Leo achieved one of his greatest dreams by winning the Copa America with Argentina. This victory was particularly meaningful as it was his first major international trophy with the national team. Messi's leadership and brilliant play throughout the tournament were instrumental in Argentina's success.

3. Olympics In 2008, Leo Messi represented Argentina in the Beijing Olympics. He played a crucial role in leading his team to victory, winning the gold medal. This achievement is a proud moment in his career, showcasing his talent on the international stage.

4. All-Star Games and Special Matches Leo has been invited to numerous all-star games and special matches throughout his career. These games bring together the best players from around the world, and Messi's participation is always a highlight. His skills and charisma make him a fan favorite at these events.

Memorable Matches and Moments

1. El Clásico Dominance Leo Messi's performances in El Clásico, the fierce rivalry between Barcelona and Real Madrid, are legendary. He has scored more goals in this fixture than any other player, and his memorable hat-tricks and game-winning goals have repeatedly thrilled fans.

2. Champions League Final 2011 In the 2011 Champions League final against Manchester United, Leo scored a brilliant goal and was instrumental in Barcelona's 3-1 victory. His performance earned him the Man of the Match award and further cemented his legacy as one of the greatest players of all time.

3. 2012: The Record-Breaking Year The year 2012 was magical for Leo Messi. He broke Gerd Müller's long-standing record by scoring 91 goals in a single calendar year. This record is a testament to his extraordinary consistency and goal-scoring prowess.

Leo's Incredible Stats

Here are some of Leo Messi's most impressive statistics:

- **World cup:** 1.
- **La Liga Titles:** 10.
- **Champions League Titles:** 4.
- **Copa del Rey Wins:** 7.
- **Ballon d'Or Wins:** 7.
- **Goals in a Calendar Year:** 91 (in 2012).
- **Hat-Tricks in La Liga:** Over 36.
- **Goals for Argentina:** 109.
- **Copa America Wins:** 1 (in 2021).
- **Olympic Gold Medals:** 1 (in 2008).
- **Goals for Barcelona:** Over 670 goals.

These numbers are more than just statistics; they represent the dedication, hard work, and passion Leo has for the game of soccer.

Each goal, each title, and each award is a testament to his incredible talent and his unwavering commitment to excellence.

Inspirational Comebacks

Leo Messi's career has not been without its challenges. He has faced injuries, tough losses, and intense competition. But each time, he has come back stronger. His resilience and determination to overcome obstacles are truly inspiring.

For instance, after suffering a hamstring injury in the 2013-2014 season, many doubted whether he could return to his best form. However, Leo worked tirelessly on his recovery, showing incredible discipline and dedication. He came back stronger, leading Barcelona to more victories and continuing to break records.

Sponsorship Deals and Media Features

Leo Messi's success on the field has also translated into lucrative sponsorship deals and media features. He has been the face of Adidas, one of the biggest sports brands in the world, for many years. His endorsement deal with Adidas is one of the largest in sports history, earning him millions of dollars annually.

Messi has also been featured in numerous commercials, documentaries, and magazine covers. His story has been told in various media formats, inspiring fans and aspiring athletes around the world. His humility, hard work, and incredible talent make him a role model for millions.

Leo Messi's career is filled with remarkable achievements, record-breaking moments, and unforgettable performances. His journey from a young boy in Rosario to a global soccer icon is a testament to his talent, dedication, and love for the game. As you continue reading about Leo's incredible journey, you'll see how his achievements have shaped his legacy and inspired millions of fans worldwide.

Conclusion: "The Final Whistle: Reflecting on Greatness"

As we come to the end of this book about Leo Messi, let's take a moment to reflect on his incredible journey. Messi's story is truly inspirational, from his humble beginnings in Rosario, Argentina, to becoming one of the greatest soccer players of all time. We've explored his early life, his rise to stardom, his record-breaking achievements, and his life off the field.

One of the key takeaways from Messi's journey is the importance of hard work and dedication. Messi never gave up on his dream despite facing numerous challenges, including a growth hormone deficiency. His relentless work ethic and determination helped him overcome obstacles and achieve greatness. This teaches us that we can overcome any challenge and reach our goals with perseverance and a positive attitude.

Another important lesson from Messi's story is the value of humility and kindness. Despite his immense success, Messi remains humble and down-to-earth.

He treats everyone with respect and uses his fame to help others through his charitable work. This shows us that true greatness is not just about talent but also about the kind of person you are.

Finally, Messi's love for his family and passion for the game are evident in everything he does. He shows us that having a solid support system and doing what you love can bring joy and fulfillment in life.

Thank you for reading this book and joining us on this journey through Leo Messi's life. We hope you've found his story as inspiring and uplifting as we have. Remember, like Messi, you, too, can achieve great things with hard work, kindness, and a love for what you do. Keep believing in yourself, chase your dreams, and never give up. Good luck, and all the best in your own journey!

Don't forget the trivia section and timeline coming up next - test your knowledge, impress your friends and family, and see who knows the most about Simone!

Thank you for reading!

Leo Messi Trivia Challenge

Test your knowledge with these 30 trivia questions about Leo Messi! Choose the correct answer from the options provided for each question.

Many of these are contained in this book. Some aren't - so you might know them already, or you might learn something new.

Test yourself, test your family, and try these out on your friends to find out who is the biggest Leo Messi Expert!

The answers are at the end.

1. Where was Leo Messi born?
    - ○ A. Buenos Aires
    - ○ B. Rosario
    - ○ C. Cordoba

2. What is Leo Messi's full first name?
    - ○ A. Lionel
    - ○ B. Leon
    - ○ C. Leonardo

3. At what age did Messi join FC Barcelona's youth academy, La Masia?
    - ○ A. 10
    - ○ B. 12
    - ○ C. 13

4. What medical condition did Leo Messi face as a child?
    - ○ A. Asthma
    - ○ B. Growth hormone deficiency
    - ○ C. Diabetes

5. Who was Leo Messi's first youth coach at Newell's Old Boys?
   - A. Ernesto Vecchio
   - B. Pep Guardiola
   - C. Diego Maradona

6. What nickname did Messi earn because of his small size and quick movements?
   - A. La Pulga
   - B. El Toro
   - C. El Gato

7. In what year did Messi make his official debut for FC Barcelona's senior team?
   - A. 2002
   - B. 2004
   - C. 2006

8. How many Ballon d'Or awards has Messi won?
   - A. 5
   - B. 6
   - C. 7

9. Which club did Messi score his first official goal for FC Barcelona against?

   o   A. Real Madrid

   o   B. Albacete

   o   C. Valencia

10. What is the nickname of the famous attacking trio Messi was part of at Barcelona?

   o   A. BBC

   o   B. MSN

   o   C. ABC

11. In what year did Messi set the record for the most goals scored in a calendar year?

   o   A. 2011

   o   B. 2012

   o   C. 2013

12. How many goals did Messi score to set the calendar year record?

   o   A. 85

   o   B. 91

   o   C. 99

13. Which Argentine city did Messi grow up in?

    ○ A. Rosario

    ○ B. Mendoza

    ○ C. Salta

14. What is the name of Messi's wife?

    ○ A. Sofia

    ○ B. Antonela

    ○ C. Maria

15. How many children do Messi and his wife have?

    ○ A. 2

    ○ B. 3

    ○ C. 4

16. What is the name of Messi's foundation?

    ○ A. Leo Messi Foundation

    ○ B. Messi's Dreams

    ○ C. Future Stars Foundation

17. In which year did Messi win his first Copa America with Argentina?

   ○ A. 2019

   ○ B. 2020

   ○ C. 2021

18. How many goals did Messi score in his first season with FC Barcelona's senior team?

   ○ A. 6

   ○ B. 9

   ○ C. 12

19. Which brand is Messi famously associated with for his sponsorship deals?

    o   A. Nike

    o   B. Adidas

    o   C. Puma

20. Which youth club did Messi first play for?

    o   A. Grandoli

    o   B. Newell's Old Boys

    o   C. Boca Juniors

21. What is Messi's jersey number for the Argentine national team?

    o   A. 7

    o   B. 10

    o   C. 11

22. In what year did Messi win his first Ballon d'Or?

    o   A. 2009

    o   B. 2010

    o   C. 2011

23. How many hat-tricks has Messi scored in La Liga?
    - ○   A. 30
    - ○   B. 36
    - ○   C. 40

24. Which famous player did Messi meet in 2013?
    - ○   A. Diego Maradona
    - ○   B. Pope Francis
    - ○   C. Pele

25. Which of Messi's relatives also became professional soccer players?
    - ○   A. His brothers
    - ○   B. His cousins
    - ○   C. His father

26. What award did Messi win at the 2014 FIFA World Cup?
    - ○   A. Golden Boot
    - ○   B. Golden Glove
    - ○   C. Golden Ball

27. Which year did Messi start his own clothing line?

   ○ A. 2016

   ○ B. 2019

   ○ C. 2020

28. How many Olympic gold medals has Messi won?

   ○ A. 1

   ○ B. 2

   ○ C. 3

29. What is the name of Messi's first son?

   ○ A. Mateo

   ○ B. Ciro

   ○ C. Thiago

30. Which charity work is Messi known for supporting?

   ○ A. Education and healthcare for children

   ○ B. Environmental conservation

   ○ C. Animal welfare

Answers

1. **B - Rosario.** Leo Messi was born in Rosario, Argentina, where he began his journey to becoming a soccer legend.

2. **A - Lionel.** Leo Messi's full first name is Lionel, although he is famously known as Leo.

3. **C - 13.** Leo joined FC Barcelona's youth academy, La Masia, at the age of 13, moving from Argentina to Spain.

4. **B - Growth hormone deficiency.** Leo faced a growth hormone deficiency as a child, a challenge he overcame with treatment.

5. **A - Ernesto Vecchio.** Ernesto Vecchio was Leo's first youth coach at Newell's Old Boys and played a significant role in his early development.

6. **A - La Pulga.** Messi earned the nickname "La Pulga," which means "The Flea," because of his small size and quick movements.

7. **B - 2004.** Messi made his official debut for FC Barcelona's senior team in 2004, marking the start of an illustrious career.

8. **C - 7.** Leo Messi has won the Ballon d'Or seven times, more than any other player in history.

9. **B - Albacete.** Leo scored his first official goal for FC Barcelona against Albacete.

10. **B - MSN.** The famous attacking trio at Barcelona, consisting of Messi, Suarez, and Neymar, was known as MSN.

11. **B - 2012.** Messi set the record for the most goals scored in a calendar year in 2012.

12. **B - 91.** Leo scored an incredible 91 goals in 2012, breaking the previous record.

13. **A - Rosario.** Leo Messi grew up in Rosario, Argentina, where he developed his love for soccer.

14. **B - Antonela.** Leo's wife is Antonela Roccuzzo, his childhood sweetheart.

15. **B - 3.** Messi and Antonela have three children: Thiago, Mateo, and Ciro.

16. **A - Leo Messi Foundation.** Leo established the Leo Messi Foundation to support access to education and healthcare for children.

17. **C - 2021.** Messi won his first Copa America with Argentina in 2021, a significant achievement in his international career.

18. **A - 6.** Messi scored six goals in his first season with FC Barcelona's senior team.

19. **B - Adidas.** Messi is famously associated with Adidas for his sponsorship deals.

20. **A - Grandoli.** Leo's first youth club was Grandoli, where he began his soccer journey.

21. **B - 10.** Messi wears the number 10 jersey for the Argentine national team.

22. **A - 2009.** Leo won his first Ballon d'Or in 2009.

23. **B - 36.** Messi holds the record for the most hat-tricks in La Liga, with over 36 hat-tricks.

24. **B - Pope Francis.** In 2013, Messi met Pope Francis, who is also from Argentina.

25. **B - His cousins.** Messi's cousins, Maximiliano and Emanuel Biancucchi, also became professional soccer players.

26. **C - Golden Ball.** Messi won the Golden Ball as the best player at the 2014 FIFA World Cup.

27. **B - 2019.** Leo Messi started his own clothing line in 2019.

28. **A - 1.** Messi has won one Olympic gold medal at the 2008 Beijing Olympics.

29. **C - Thiago.** Leo's first son is named Thiago Messi.

30. **A** - Education and healthcare for children. Through his foundation, Leo supports education and healthcare for children.

Congratulations on completing the Leo Messi Trivia Challenge! How many did you get right?

Now you know even more about the incredible journey and achievements of one of the greatest soccer players in history.

Leo Messi's Journey: Key Milestones

Here's a timeline of some of the most iconic, important, and influential milestones in Leo Messi's life (so far!):

June 24, 1987 - Leo Messi is born in Rosario, Argentina.

1992 - At age 5, Messi starts playing soccer at a local club, Grandoli, coached by his father, Jorge Messi.

1995 - At age 8, Messi joins Newell's Old Boys, a prestigious soccer club in Rosario.

1998 - Diagnosed with a growth hormone deficiency at age 11.

2000 - At age 13, Messi moves to Spain with his family to join FC Barcelona's youth academy, La Masia.

November 16, 2003 - Makes his unofficial debut for FC Barcelona in a friendly match against Porto.

October 16, 2004 - Makes his official debut for FC Barcelona's senior team in a La Liga match against Espanyol.

May 1, 2005 - Scores his first official goal for FC Barcelona against Albacete, becoming the youngest scorer in the club's history at that time.

June 2005 - Leads Argentina's U-20 team to victory in the FIFA U-20 World Cup, winning both the Golden Shoe and Golden Ball awards.

May 17, 2006 - Wins his first UEFA Champions League title with Barcelona.

August 2008 - Wins an Olympic gold medal with Argentina at the Beijing Olympics.

December 1, 2009 - Wins his first Ballon d'Or award.

May 2009 - Helps Barcelona achieve a historic treble by winning La Liga, Copa del Rey, and UEFA Champions League in the same season.

January 2010 - Wins his second Ballon d'Or award.

December 2012 - Sets a world record by scoring 91 goals in a single calendar year.

March 2013 - Meets Pope Francis, also from Argentina, in the Vatican.

July 2014 - Leads Argentina to the FIFA World Cup final, winning the Golden Ball as the tournament's best player.

June 2015 - Wins his fourth UEFA Champions League title with Barcelona, completing another treble season.

June 30, 2017 - Marries his childhood sweetheart, Antonela Roccuzzo.

October 2017 - Becomes the all-time top scorer in La Liga.

August 2019 - Launches his own clothing line, "Messi."

July 2021 - Wins his first major international trophy with Argentina by securing the Copa America title.

December 18, 2022 - Captains Argentina to victory in the FIFA World Cup, winning the tournament and being awarded the Golden Ball as the best player of the competition.

This timeline highlights the significant milestones and achievements in Leo Messi's life and career, showcasing his journey from a young soccer enthusiast in Rosario to a global soccer icon.

Claim Your Free Bonus Coloring Book

A free bonus coloring book download is waiting for you as a thank you for picking up this book. We think you'll like it.

Just scan the QR code below or visit
ColorCraftBooks.com/colorcraft-bonus.

Kids: Make sure to ask a parent first! ●

Scan to get your free coloring book download.

Thanks for reading.

Would you help us with a review?

If you enjoyed the book, we'd be so grateful if you could help us by leaving a review on Amazon (even a super short one!). Reviews help us so much - in spreading the word, in helping others decide if the book is right for them, and as feedback for our team.

If you'd like to give us any suggestions, need help with something, or to find more books like this, please visit us at ColorCraftBooks.com.

Thank you

Thank you so much for picking up *All About Leo Messi*. We really hope you enjoyed it and learned a lot about this extraordinary athlete.

Thanks again,

The Color Craft team

Made in the USA
Las Vegas, NV
17 December 2024

14482821R10049